Dedicated to ...

All who have come before me, those who stand beside me, and the few who follow me.

counting the days

Preface

August 11th, 1998, was the day I began my existence— the eldest of four children to my parents and one of eighteen grandchildren to my grandparents. My childhood was that of a simple one, enveloped with love, strength, and wisdom from all around me. Although there was much joy and happiness in my childhood, I have had my share of despair, loss, and sadness. During these times, the inspiration to author pieces rose to the surface of my being and colored the following pages.

These colors changed to mimic seasons where my summers would be warm, springs would be vibrant, winter would be solemn, and fall would be filled with passion. My aspirations to write originated early in my youth as I learned of meaningful narratives, powerful haikus, and whimsical fantasies that touched not only my heart but evermore my soul. I quickly noticed that I paid considerably more attention in my English class than in any other class on my roster. Learning about writing styles, formats, and variations intrigued me enough to begin authoring pieces myself.

This book contains all the pieces I have created from childhood until now. Please remember that they are far from perfect and come from places of emotion and experience. I hope that at least one piece resonates with you as you read through. I offer my warmest thanks to all those who have supported me throughout my journey in life, and I wish them the most extraordinary embrace from the universe and its pleasures.

"What lies before you and what lies ahead of you, pale in comparison to what lies within you."

Ralph Waldo Emerson

counting the days

Day 1

His breath on my chest.

The sun as it pierces through the curtains.

The taste of hazelnut in my coffee.

The subtle aroma of clean linens.

A dog's bark.

Love.

These are the feelings in my heart.

Day 2

Rise gentle sun and shed your light,
Awaken the sunflower and bring me delight.
Birth a sunflower and bestow it with beauty,
Then one day present her to me.
A sunflower that chooses me among others,
A sunflower that is adorned by mother and sisters and lovers.
One that stays through the storms of desperation.
One that smiles with radiance.
Rise gentle sun and shed your light,
Awaken the sunflower and bring me delight.

counting the days

Day 3

I hope that one day,
You happen to glance into the mirror,
and see the beautiful person,
I got to see every day.

Day 4

It has been much too long
since I have known my why.
To what purpose gives you such endless reason?
To be free or shackled.
Ah, yes, how could I ever forget?
That purpose,
Exists in *their* eyes as they look up to me,
Dwelling in their smiles as they reminisce,
Fluttering in their hearts as they know my love.
It was in *them*,
That I discovered my why.

Day 5

The moment I saw you holding his hand
was the exact moment I no longer loved you.
You had become a fleeting memory.
A chapter that ended too soon.
Feelings of love turned to angst.
Platitudes of belief, support, and loyalty
left at the doorway
as you took your final steps away.

Day 6

Our lives are like books; someone is bound to come along and read every chapter of your lore. Don't regret its contents, and don't fear sharing your chapters. With every passing season, a new chapter forms, giving birth to a myriad of experiences, emotions, challenges, and lessons, all of which mold you into the person you are today.

Each story is more unique than the last. Our memories catalog our discoveries and feelings, which we share only with those we deem "worthy enough." Within ourselves, we reread these chapters to basque in nostalgia or to prescribe pearls of wisdom to those who seek it. Many fear their stories being read by others because they're either ashamed of their past or have not accepted it for what it is. Fret not, for those who peruse your chapters will only see the reasons why you are a legend standing before them today.

This is your story, your myth, your folklore

and *you* are the main character!

Day 7

O' the mighty have fallen...
An angel plummeting from the stars.
Wings torn, forsaken of pride.
The fiery Earth absorbs its plunge.

Produced from the smoldering embers,
Embodied within a veil of smoke,
Ascended a mortal of flesh and blood.

Rebirthed with an enlivened will,
Their spirit is unshakable.
Their desire is insatiable.
Their passion is voracious.

You are this angel...

This life was not one of your choosing,
Nor did you elicit your suffering.
Nevertheless... This life is yours.

Just as a phoenix rises from its ashes,
You, too, shall rise.
Head held high, ambitions that pierces the clouds.

Bolster your spirit.
Seek that which you desire.
Inspire through your passion.
The mighty may have fallen...

Relentlessly, you will rise yet again.

<u>Day 8</u>

I am afraid of the dark.

It's not the type of dark, similar to turning the lights out, and you can't see anything. It's the version of darkness, similar to the night sky becoming an endless void and swallowing you whole.

Space travel would be out of the question for me. Not for the fact that I would traverse the nothingness of space but solely because of the sheer uncertainty. The lack of control is nothing short of terrifying, with limitless possibilities of floating across the vast deep.

In these times when I am petrified by fear, I place every ounce of my trust in you. My faith in you overflows with enough bravery to transcend the stars without hesitation. This trust in you carries with it all the hopes for our future.

                                                   A future with you.

counting the days

Day 9

If I could fly,

I would fly up.

Up, where the clouds have no limits.

Up, where the sun shines the brightest.

Up, where space contains the cosmos.

Up, where freedom...

Is all I find.

__Day 10__

A parent says to their son...
A sibling says to their brother...
A spouse says to their husband...

A little boy with dreams crushed by expectation.
A teenager copes with society.
A gay man chasing after his father's shadow.
An old man killed by the very demons he never parted with.

Being a man carries with it a share of expectations and stigmas,
Being a man requires the strength to push on,
Being a man means giving respect even when it's not reciprocated,
Being a man makes you wrong, no matter the circumstance.

Is this truly what it means to "Be a man?"

counting the days

Day 11

I looked up at the sky,
saw an ocean of blue,
and felt so alone.

Day 12

She stood before me...

As she held my hands,

Tears fell from her eyes.

Her mouth uttered, "I am sorry."

Gazing at her, I replied,

"Now, I only see through you."

Then, without hesitation...

I walked away.

counting the days

Day 13

When i tell you, *"I love your eyes."*

i mean,

i love how your soul
refracts itself through your irises
like the sun as it bounces its rays
off the ocean surface.

Day 14

If someone calls upon you,

No matter what they've done or said,

Extend your hand unto them.

Offer your shoulder so they may cry.

You may never know,

If you were their final hope,

Before ultimately giving up.

Day 15

Never forget just how much,
I love you.
Regardless of the words we exchange,
the distances that separate us,
and every moment that becomes a memory.

                        I will always love you.

Day 16

Those who smile the brightest

are also the ones who cry alone.

They laugh to lighten the atmosphere,

Only to be greeted by depression as they lie in bed.

They are present for anyone and everyone,

Even when no one is there for them.

Those who smile the brightest

are the strongest.

counting the days

Day 17

If I whispered in your ear,

"I want to die."

Would your heart break for me?
Would your hands reach out for mine?
Would your arms embrace me?
Would your ears register the pain in my voice?
Would you try to stop me?
Would you let me go?

If I whispered in your ear,

"I want to die..."

__Day 18__

If I am being honest, it wasn't love at first sight.

Instead, I was fascinated by you

and took the time to hear all of your interests.

Watched how you carried yourself.

Experienced your passions.

That was the moment I realized just how deeply rooted

my love for you became.

Day 19

The happiest people,
Never brag about it,
They always take their time,
They stop to smell the roses,
They've learned that tolerance does not equal patience,
They've discovered that kindness trumps pettiness,
They've uncovered how to smile,
Even when their world crumbles around them.

Day 20

The last lesson I ever learned from you,
was not to care too much.
Because when I care too much,
I only end up getting hurt again.

counting the days

Day 21

you will forever be the very first thing on my mind,

when i wake up.

the very last thing on my mind,

when i go to sleep.

and the only thing on my mind,

as i go about my day.

that has never changed.

Day 22

The belt wrapped around your neck.
The gun, cradled in your mouth, finger on the trigger.
The razor resting above your wrist.
The pills offer eternal comfort from their bottle.

Such a commitment ensures specific results.

All your pain will come to an end.
People will know of your untimely exit from this life.
The stressors that once shackled you will be removed.
The weight of the world will no longer rest on your shoulders.

With all that said... Consider...

Your parents will know they have failed you.
Your significant other will never embrace your warmth.
Your siblings will endure worse pain than you were.
Your friends will endlessly blame themselves for not seeing it sooner.

Those who loved you now have to remember you longer than they knew you.

Life, as you know it, may be strangling you.
It may be forcing you to choose between life and death.
Should you find yourself at these crossroads...

Choose life, choose pain, and choose the struggle.
You will triumph, you will evolve, and,
You... will... live...

Learn from it so that you, too, can save someone from depravity.

counting the days

Day 23

If it turns out that today is your last day
and you do not wake up tomorrow,
Would you be proud of who you've become?
Would you be content with leaving this world behind?
Would you have any last words?

Day 24

Over time, I realized I'm no one's forever.

    I'm merely the stop before your train reaches its destination.

The bridge you take to cross the river.

    The handrail you use when going up the stairs.

A shoulder to cry on when you feel sad.

    A stepping stone to be walked on.

I will build you up, only to watch you leave.

    A lighthouse that guides ships in the darkness.

Day 25

i was pretty lost before i met you
it was like swimming in a never-ending ocean
rather quickly;
you became my life raft.
now...
i have to remember how to swim
without you.

counting the days

Day 26

And just like that,
I remembered.
How to fake my smile,
again.

Day 27

"It is what it is"
Will be the very words
that are scattered to the wind
with my ashes.

Day 28

How could one thing that once illuminated the brightest colors slowly paint streaks of grey across the canvas over time?

I stood in the depths of nowhere as the sand rolled past my feet, peering up at the night sky and watching flickers of light fly toward me. It was as though missiles were being dropped on my head, and my body was frozen in place, fearing the unknown.

I drag a hit from my vape.

Steadily allowing the cancer to branch itself throughout my lungs, I exhale a cloud of smoke. Breathing had become a chore that my mother constantly nagged me about. Sleeping became an impossible task without guzzling untold amounts of pills to aid the process. Smiling became a dream I once had as a child but an unobtainable reality.

"Is any of this worth it?"

Blessed with patience, I'll find out eventually. By the time I get those answers, it'll be too late.

Day 29

As the sun sets and ignites the horizon,

would you stand by my side?

we could watch the stars through each other's eyes.

or revel in the melancholy,

as we hold each other.

Never letting go.

Day 30

> I once asked a little boy,
> *"What do you want to be when you grow up?"*

"To be loved,"
He replied.

counting the days

Day 31

Do you think it would be okay?

If I didn't have any more "tomorrows?"

Day 32

The blame has always been mine to bear.

I broke my own heart,

expecting you to love me the same way,

I loved you.

Day 33

Happiness has always chased me,

> I have always been faster.

Day 34

~~You are worth it.~~

~~You are valued.~~

~~You are important.~~

~~You are loved.~~

~~You are enough.~~

You never mattered.

Day 35

Just like that...

> **We're strangers again.**

Day 36

Slowly, I walked toward you
extending my arms to embrace
every bit of you.

In that breathless moment,
I forgot about all of the pain.

Day 37

Never fall in love with the same person twice.

The second time, you will only fall in love with,

the memories,

the nostalgia,

the little things,

the past.

Day 38

The truest form of love,

always ends up,

hurting you the most.

Day 39

Whenever you *miss* me,
Let it be nostalgic, not painful.

> Remember,
> how I'd comb my fingers through you hair
> when you felt like life was too much.

Remember,
how I'd gently kiss your forehead
and you'd feel at peace.

> Remember,
> how I'd hold you closely at night
> to make sure you never fell asleep alone.

Whenever you *miss* me,
I hope you miss the memories of "us."

Day 40

Just in case no one ever told you...

It's okay to – cry.
— feel lonely.
— scream.
— feel helpless.
— lose it.
— feel sad.
— disappear.
— feel lost.
— not be okay.

But it's not okay to stay that way...

Day 41

If you ever find yourself

thinking you should settle in life.

Fight it.

The moment you give in,

You will never find the joy that you seek.

Day 42

Be ever so still.

Stay ever so silent.

                      For death will wash over you,

                            like a calm wave,

                            breaking upon the shore.

counting the days

__Day 43__

If you love them.

More than you love yourself.

You already made a mistake.

<u>Day 44</u>

If you ever desire to leave me,
i will not stop you.

      Some people are like,
        leafs that fall from a tree.

            Throughout the seasons,
              one falls after another.

     Should your time come, and you must go,
           then go.

Just know, I never forget,
those who leave.

Day 45

No matter the pain,
No matter the sorrow,
Your sun,
will always rise tomorrow.

__Day 46__

I have journeyed this land.

> My feet took me to the sea.
> My eyes took me to the forest.
> My ears took me atop a mountain.
> My mind took me to the ocean.
> My heart...
> My heart took me to you.

> > I have journeyed this land, and yet,
> > My soul tied itself to yours.

Day 47

Doorway

Long ago, I attempted suicide. Few knew about it, and far fewer understood my pain and sorrow. Although it was a failed attempt, what was left behind was a scar that has never faded. I see this scar when I look in the mirror; I feel it as I wash my body in the shower; it cradles me to sleep every night. This is my depression.

So much time has passed since it began; over that time, it grew into a lifestyle I became accustomed to. I am unsure when it first came to be, but it affected everything I do before I knew it. Depression is a senseless cancer that infects all aspects of who you are down to your very core. Such a thing empties all positive emotions and emphasizes all negative ones. For those who just discovered their depression, it can be all-consuming and ever so controlling. However, for professionals like me, it fills your background like a shadow that never leaves your side.

Do not misunderstand; the life I live is nothing short of gay and jovial. I just thought I would give those who wondered a gateway into what I see through my eyes daily. Most mornings, I wake up shadowed by loneliness, only to be comforted by the warmth of water as I shower. After I prepare myself for what that day offers, I recline within the thought that "one should not look for Love as it will find you when you least expect it." Throughout the day, I keep as busy as possible to avoid thoughts of self-hatred and loathing, which is successful for the most part. I try to stay late at work if possible because I fear that no one will greet me when I return "home," which is far too consuming. Nevertheless, I

counting the days

go "home." Returning to such a place grants me no satisfaction as I am crippled by the darkness that looms across the scenery. I am confronted by a bed that is ever so cold and has become my only comfort. Sleep is the key to this endlessness, a sort of escape from the bounds of reality. I sit in the kitchen watching my grandfather cook. My family surrounds me, and I can still feel her lips as they touch mine. My eyes open in no time, and the cycle begins again.

One thought never leaves my mind: "When I die, who will attend my funeral, and what will be said about me?" As painful as that may be to some, those who know me closely will understand that that will be when I can finally feel relieved. I can only hope that when people talk of me, they do so with smiles, and there will be stories about how I was anything but ordinary. Normalcy is never remembered; therefore, I chose to be outspoken, brutally honest, and, best of all, weird. For some reason, these traits are ones that no one can easily forget. Honestly, I can say I took full advantage of that fact. Looking back, I have not lived a poor life nor have any reason to be as gloomy as I am. To those who find my death too much to bear, I offer you this: look up toward the vastness of the night sky, and the first star that catches your eye is nothing but me reaching out for you as I always have.

Godspeed

Day 48

Turning Tables

Cameron always walked through life with his head held high no matter what had happened to him, regardless of the emotions he felt. He made a habit of forcing others out of his life to avoid any unnecessary sadness or heartache. His motto is, "Cut them off before they ever get the chance to cut me off." It was a somber existence to everyone else, but to him, it had grown into an uncontrollable habit. It was one of his many preventative measures to ensure he would never allow someone to take advantage of his gentle heart. Habits are not spontaneous; they are borne from scars.

At the juvenile age of nineteen, Cameron had devoted the entirety of his love to a man only to be left naked, bruised, and alone. Just as in any normal relationship, the man continuously showered Cameron with attention, care, and safety. Somewhere along the way, the man told Cameron,

"If you love me, then you'll have sex with me and my friends."

Cameron agreed to do so without hesitation because when he loved, he loved hard. Shortly thereafter, sex with him and his friends turned into just sex with his friends and then friends of the friends. The first time Cameron attempted to leave the man, he was beaten and bound. Treated as though he was property devoid of fundamental human rights, this existence had been forced upon him for three long years. In fear of reparations, Cameron abandoned his family and severed all ties at the man's discretion. Cameron had made an impromptu visit to his grandmother, whom he adored above anyone, and one thing she told him would change his life for years.

> *"A seed grows without sound, but a tree falls with a huge noise. Destruction is loud, but creation is quiet. This is the power of silence... grow silently, my boy."*

Shocked by this realization, Cameron was inspired to do whatever it took to break away from him and finally gain freedom.

Freedom was something that Cameron never thought was possible, and yet, through sheer will, he had attained it. Breaking free of that man left a void in Cameron tantamount to the depth of the Mariana Trench. He had felt that although their relationship was abusive and toxic, at the very least, the man would always be there. His mentality was apparently flawed at best, and he slowly started to improve it to where he would feel deserving of actual love. Cameron sought help from a plethora of therapists, and little by little, he regained hope that his life was not comparable to property or trash.

While reading *The Dictionary of Obscure Sorrows* on the A train, someone had occupied the seat on his right. Cameron thought this was odd since the train car was pretty empty, with only a few seats being taken. Nevertheless, he continued to immerse himself further into his book, coming across the word *monachopsis,* or the subtle but persistent feeling of being out of place. This word particularly stood out to him as it accurately described how he constantly felt no matter where he was. Like a break in the silence, the person who was sitting next to him commented,

> *"What is it you're reading?"*

Making a decent effort to ignore the person, Cameron sat unphased by the passenger's question.

counting the days

"Sorry, that was rude of me; my name is Tommy. What is your name?"

Tommy exclaims.

With a deep sigh, Cameron lifted his eyes from the book to meet Tommy's. He sat there speechless, unable to help but be trapped in the light blue and green oceanic hues that composed Tommy's irises.

The awkward atmosphere eased as Tommy lifted his hand to snap his fingers. As though out of shock, Cameron blinked several times and slightly shook his head to ensure that what was before his eyes was the mind displaying a fantasy. Tommy was relatively loud and extroverted, which was the opposite of Cameron. However, Cameron saw this as a perfect opportunity to work on his socializing abilities. To shroud his embarrassment, he began talking about the first thing that came to mind.

"My grandmother gave me this book as a reminder that among our vast language, there are still words that can describe the emotions and feelings we experience."

Not knowing what type of response Tommy would give, Cameron grew nervous, as though he had said something he disliked. To his surprise, Tommy had found a curious intellect about Cameron. After further analyzing this, he had to think of an appropriate response to show Cameron he was just as interested in the conversation. A simple "That was sweet of her" or "Oh, that's interesting" would not suffice in his mind, and it was regarded as disrespectful to him.

Tommy responded,

"I have always wondered if there were actual words that could depict some of my feelings."

counting the days

Hearing this sparked a fire within Cameron; he had taken that response as an invitation to talk about something he was very enthusiastic about, which was Tommy's intention. Cameron begins to interrogate Tommy about the feelings he has experienced and corresponds them with words from his book. Undenounced, much of what he asked was related to personal and private feelings that Tommy was not typically comfortable discussing with others. This was the first instance where the walls surrounding Cameron's heart had been conquered. A bond formed within that brief exchange of words, but would Tommy be prepared for what follows?

Day 49

The Old Soul

It can be said that in time, you learn most of what you can from life, whether through mistakes, lost chances, or painful paths. The world often forgets the few individuals who live an old soul deep within themselves. Sometimes, possessing an old soul gives you a different perspective on things in life. I am one of those people. While still young, I encompassed myself with the elderly to absorb the knowledge and wisdom that they've experienced. There are things that I know and have the answers to; however, I have not yet experienced what would warrant that wisdom. It can indeed be a painful thing. It is crucial to see the potential outcomes of things without thinking about a solution.

My marriage fell apart, and my ex-wife, who still had the mindset of a child, did not understand the reality of adulthood. In turn, it is up to me to let her go and allow her to mature and grow up into a fine young woman. Although this may be opinionated, I had the knowledge and wisdom to sustain a healthy marriage, which my ex-wife had no intention of staying in. I was painfully aware of that fact, and because of it, I could predict the result. Yet I am all the more helpless but to let her explore the many suitors that await her newly granted status of "single."

counting the days

Day 50

Giving up will get you Nowhere

As you embark on your journey through life, you will be tested...

In every manner,
In every instance,
In every way.
Do not give up.

Every human faces these odds...
Where the tide is against you,
Where your sun turns ice cold,
Where your best... Simply is not enough.
Do not give up.

We all experience depression,
We all experience heartbreak,
We all experience loneliness,
We all experience sadness,
We all experience.
Do not give up.

The darkness will envelop your world, and all will seem pointless.
Once bright colors will lose their hues.
Feelings of love and joy will dull.
Tears will fall from your face as you rip your hair out.

counting the days

And your motivation to breathe will be non-existent.
Do not give up.

Always remember that these hardships,
Are nothing but temporary, and they will not last.
These moments only serve as a test.
A test of your determination, drive, and will.
They force you to your physical, mental, and spiritual limits.
Do not give up.

> Stand tall and stand resolute.
> You are unshakable,
> You are remarkable,
> You are human,
> You are perfectly imperfect.
> Do not give up.

Remember that you are the main character in your movie.
Take pride in the individual you have become.
Let go of the weights dragging you down.
Focus on the "you" you want to be.
I know it would be easier just to give up, but
Remember that giving up means that those hardships decide your future.

> Remember that giving up will get you nowhere.

Day 51

My Vault

Over time, I have come to build a vault. I have learned that when I feel negative emotions or things do not go my way, I store them within the depths of this vault. Truthfully, I do not remember the last time someone had taken the time to ask me, "Are you okay?" Not the common surface-level question nor the simple sort that prompts a bleak response. The type of "Are you okay?" where they show up at your doorstep because they noticed a change of tone in your voice or saw that the winds blew on me a little too hard that day. Realizing that this form of cognizance and care is rare, I only granted permission to bury my feelings further until I quickly became one who was no longer emotionally aware.

Pondering my actions to result in such a travesty took an untold amount of time from my life. Time otherwise better spent on possibly seeking therapy to unravel the scrolls of traumas and feelings that, one day, will come to bear their fangs. What was it that people began to think I was genuinely okay? Was it the smiles they wore when I reassured them? Was it in their laughter after I said something funny? Was it possibly in their tears as I held them during troubled times? I had gotten so accustomed to being there for everyone that I lost sight of what it meant to allow myself to experience those same emotions. It was like helping someone bring in their grocery bags, only to take them with me afterward. Somewhere along the way, those I considered to be in my close circle slowly withdrew.

I do not blame those who choose themselves, nor do I harbor any ill will because of it. However, I will say that when someone finally does come along and asks me, "Are you okay?" out of genuine care and curiosity, the floodgates to my vault may open with full force.

Day 52

Imagine

As I gaze up at the clouds, I realize just how beautiful the world is beyond these windows. Sometimes, I wonder how people can walk this Earth every day without noticing all of the beauties that are held out there. From the color of the sky to the brisk and fresh scent of the ocean breeze, we take for granted these natural wonders and label them as "ordinary." When, in fact, these wonders are anything but.

The wind blew hard this afternoon as though attempting to tell me something important. I wonder what it could have been or if it was all a part of my imagination because I am going insane. Both are plausible, but which is more likely to be the case? At this point, I am merely taking note of my thoughts and ideas that so generously waft around in my head. One of these days, I would like to wake up somewhere along the coastline and sit outside on my porch, sipping on a hot cup of coffee. Imagining a picturesque scene like that is almost enough to give me a much-needed mental break from my current surroundings. However, life is never so easy to let you take such a vacation.

I am in the military, and being in the military means you are always away from wherever or whatever you call "home." They ship you off to be hundreds, if not thousands, of miles away to fill a slot and slave for an organization that claims to fight for our freedoms. In most instances, that claim is true, but under the wrong administration, that line can quickly blur into needless strife.

Day 53

Bottle the Pain

    I cried today. Sitting naked in the bathtub in the fetal position with a half-drunken bottle of Crown resting on the edge. Time passed as though it was a mere illusion, and maybe that was for the better. Crying over events that transpired throughout my life, mainly those I never got closure on. The memory of my shower will forever remain one of the most vivid.

    Scalding water embraced my body with the warmth it never received from those who left me. An unhealthy amount of alcohol circulated through my system to force me to forget the pain and suffering they put me through. They isolated within the four corners of my tub to avoid realizing that the emptiness of my apartment solidified my loneliness. My fingers shrivel just like my heart every time someone abandons me. Tears cascaded from my bloodshot and puffy eyes, only to be camouflaged by falling water. In those moments, I feel nothing and everything at once.

    When did that life turn into this? My childhood was happy, and I never feared to display and share my emotions. Somewhere along my path, I developed the inability to properly cope with all of the negative emotions that I feel. It's as though I bottle them, seal them tight, and store them away in the depths of my heart. Over the years, I've refused to allow myself to process these feelings, which inevitably come back to bite me. I have an expansive tolerance; however, everyone has their boiling point. Every time I reach mine, I degrade into a shell of my extroverted self to prepare for the impending weight of depression.

Day 54

Value to Teach Your Child

Over the years, I have come to learn a great deal of things from both my father and many others whom I've considered father figures. Here is an ever-evolving list of values I learned and plan to teach my son, children, and grandchildren. Please remember that this is undoubtedly not an exclusive list of values but a culmination of lessons I've garnered thus far. The meaning behind each value varies from person to person. Therefore, I implore you to search for your meaning within these words.

- *Never shake a person's hand sitting down*

- *In a negotiation, never make the first offer*

- *Request the late checkout*

- *Thank a veteran, then make it up to them*

- *When entrusted with a secret, keep it*

- *Hold your heroes to a higher standard*

- *Return a borrowed car with a full tank of gas*

- *Play with passion or don't play at all*

- *Every person is unique; let them be who they want to be*

- *Try writing your eulogy and never stop revising it*

- *Stand up to bullies. Protect those bullied*

counting the days

- *Be confident yet humble*
- *Never be afraid to ask out the best-looking girl/boy in the room*
- *Be who you are, regardless of others' opinions*
- *Be like a duck, calm on the surface, and paddle like hell underneath*
- *When you marry the girl/boy, you marry their family but never forget about yours*
- *After writing an angry email, letter, or text, read it carefully, then delete it*
- *Manners maketh the person*
- *Give credit, take blame*
- *It's okay to cry. Showing emotion <u>does not</u> make you weak*
- *If you need help, seek it; don't take it on alone*
- *Eat lunch with the new kid*
- *Don't let a wishbone grow where a backbone should be*
- *When shaking someone's hand, grip firmly and look them in the eyes*
- *First, experience the serenity of loneliness before committing to another*
- Win humbly and lose gracefully

Day 55

To the only boy I ever loved

Everything he has given me has added volume to the best parts of my life and created opportunities for my future that never would have appeared had he not become an integral role. I can say only so many things accurately convey my sheer adoration, admiration, respect, and love for the man I call my husband.

In no time at all, he was able to secure the most considerable portion of my heart and soul, which surely scared me because of past trauma and suffering. I quickly overcame that fear with the help of the love he consistently showed me. His appearance had exposed bright hues of lilac purple across the canvas of my life.

His voice was gentle as they caressed my ears.
His touch was warm as he held my hand.
His heart was pure as he said, "I love you."

In these moments, I realized that I was no longer traveling alone in this world. I'm still uncertain of the exact instance that my heart began to flutter when I was near him. Wait... I do remember! It was the first time he gave me a peek into his reality, and let me tell you right now... What I saw gave me the strength to overcome my terrors and thrust me into the start of new beginnings, experiences, and emotions that laid a path to the rest of our futures together.

"Believe in yourself, and believe in your potential."

counting the days

These words he uttered to me when I was at my lowest shattered my insecurities and bolstered my foundation to forge ahead during my most trying times. Believing in myself was constantly a challenge I struggled to triumph over. Yet only a few words spoken from his lips carried with them enough hope and love to spark change in me. Immense pride washes over me every time I mention he's my husband.

He had become my sole priority in life, building a path for our futures that we could comfortably walk along.

He had become my soulmate in the blink of an eye, where I pictured him and our children playing at the beach.

He had become my person, one I would stand beside despite hell or high water.

On every occasion, I told him, "I love you," I expressed what I felt throughout the depths of my soul. Finally, when I look into the mirror, I see the amazing person he tells me I am.

To my husband, for it was he who gave me everything.

Day 56

Answer "no"

With every question you read below, say the answer "no" aloud.

Are you happy?

Do you feel like you are worth it?

Do you feel important enough?

Do you feel appreciated?

Now I'll ask you this, (the same rules apply)

Are you going to give up?

Are you going to let it defeat you?

Are you going to let it stop you?

Are you going to give up?

Day 57

It costs a price, but doesn't everything?

It wasn't long until I noticed they were no longer by my side. In the time it took for a heart to beat, a few words discarded the entirety of a friendship. Very little was said, and yet my darkest nightmares metamorphosed into my reality.

Looking back, we made a mistake by traveling down the road we did, and a good part of me knew that this would happen at some point in our future; however, no matter my preparedness, I could not have braced myself for the pain that would come. Abundantly in my heart, the sensation of bitterness and anguish grew to new lengths, for the loneliness I had come to know quickly sprouted into a massive tree that engulfed all of what my life had become.

Regularly, I ask myself, "Why must it be me who suffers this continued pain?" It's like I've fallen into a perpetual cycle of giving all my love to someone, who enjoys it for a season and then makes a swift exit. I highly doubt that the answer to such a simple question will ever show itself.

I once fell in love with a girl, then a boy, and finally, I came to love myself because that was all I had left.

Day 58

One day

    Sometimes I get very depressed to the point where I only want to lie in bed and do absolutely nothing. This lasts for a few days, and I lose all motivation to exist. Usually, I rarely eat during these times and find it increasingly difficult to embark upon society. Very often, I've searched for the root cause of this depression, but it seemingly makes things worse as I never come across the answer.

    Explaining it can be excruciatingly challenging, especially when someone asks me if I am okay. So, I try my best to dawn a false smile and maintain social appearances. It was always best that I avoided that situation altogether. To merely say that I was enveloped in darkness would be a casual understatement – it would be more accurate to say that everything that I feel becomes numb and non-existent. I embrace myself in the cold darkness to help pass the time, giving me less to worry about.

    I don't care to have people seeing me when I am like that, which is why I lie about it so often. As I've aged, it's steadily become one of my vulnerabilities and weaknesses. It's almost like the sun doesn't rise for several days, and the moon looms over the sky just to mock me. My world remains in a cold stillness that freezes everything it touches. It makes me yearn for death so that I don't have to try so hard to breathe. Throughout this, I tend to sleep as much as possible, trying to slip out of consciousness.

counting the days

        Displaying positive emotions to those who don't know me became very easy for me. I perfected the art of faking it.

        For as long as I can remember, attempting to fix my depression only caused it to grow worse. One day, I will fix it, and for now... That's okay with me.

Day 59

Morning thoughts

A lot of the time, death is the topic on my mind. Dying on deployment, on my way to work, in a firefight, to protect someone important to me, or even dying for a stranger. That thought always lingers in the crevices of my mind, somewhat like a shadow that never disappears.

My therapist told me I'm passively suicidal.

Videos of soldiers coming home in caskets from battles they've lost seem to frequent my social media. Foreshadowing? It's always a casket that comes off of a jet, greeted by the member's family, who are typically in tears and inconsolable, which is to be expected. I think about my death and the uncertainty of it.

Why would it have happened?

When would it happen?

Could it have been avoided?

Will I come to regret it in the next life?

So many questions will never be answered, at least in this lifetime.

counting the days

    There are a vast amount of people I have come to care for, and so many of them know I would find my death to be a solemn occasion. To prepare them, I've decided to write letters to them or hide pieces of my soul in the things I've written. For some, they'll need that extra push from me to find some sort of closure after I depart this existence. I understand that this may be unusual for someone my age to do, but those who know me would understand. My curiosity for the afterlife drives me towards the finish line of life every day.

Our futures are unwritten, so pick up a pen and start.

Here I go...

Day 60

Dust layered over the shelves,

An empty pill bottle on the floor,

A cold-lifeless body lying in bed.

As they entered his room, they realized,

he no longer had the desire,

to continue living in this world.

Disclaimer

Everything said in this book conveys genuine feelings and emotions that we all experience – if you find yourself at the crossroads of pushing forward or giving up...

Push forward like I have.

Get help and never stop fighting for yourself.

I believe in you, and I know you're worth it.